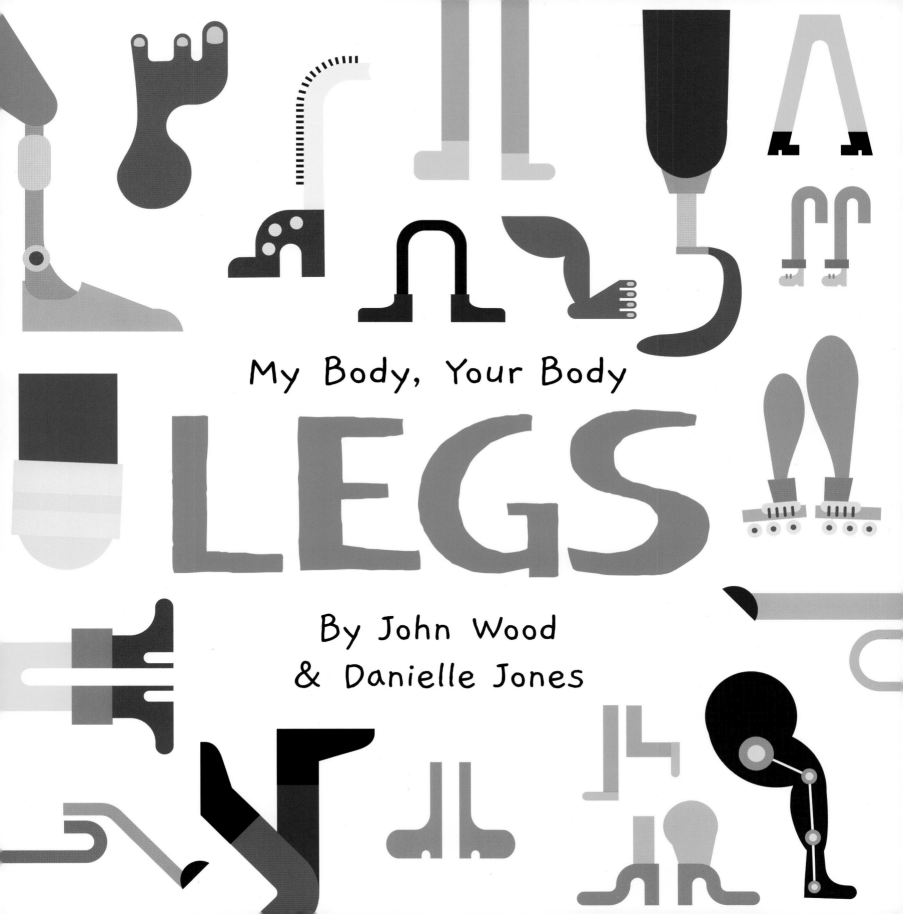

My Body, Your Body

LEGS

By John Wood
& Danielle Jones

BookLife
PUBLISHING

©2019
BookLife Publishing Ltd.
King's Lynn, Norfolk PE30 4LS

ISBN: 978-1-78637-744-9

Written by: John Wood

Edited by: Madeline Tyler

Designed by: Danielle Jones

*All facts, statistics, web addresses and URLs
in this book were verified as valid and
accurate at time of writing. No responsibility
for any changes to external websites
or references can be accepted by either
the author or publisher.*

All images are courtesy of danjazzia
via Shutterstock.com, unless otherwise
specified. With thanks to Getty Images,
Thinkstock Photo and iStockphoto.
Additional illustrations by Danielle Jones.

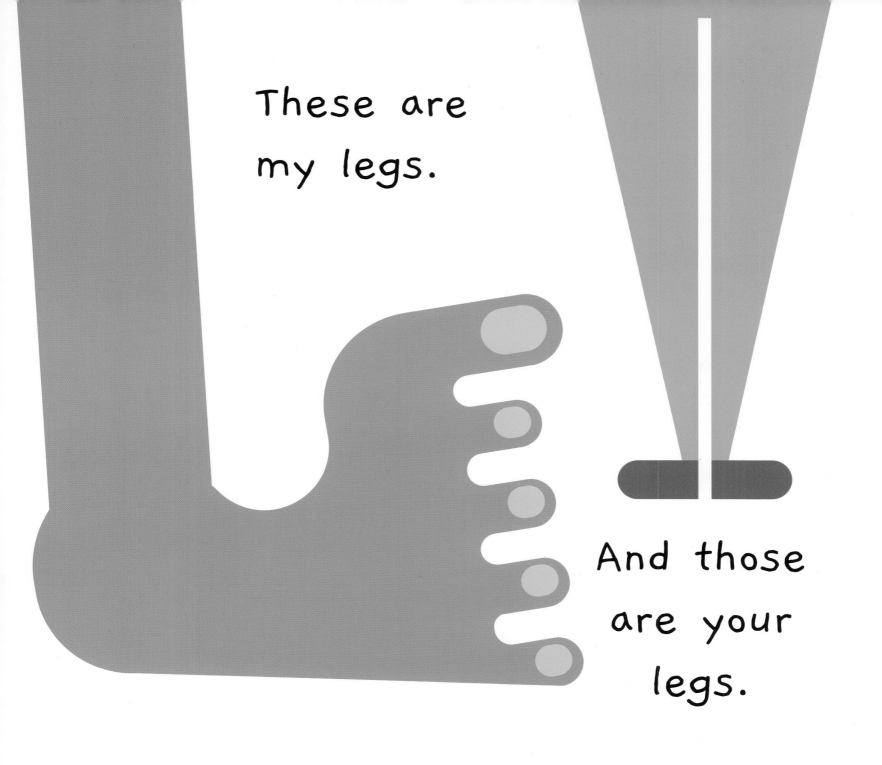

These are
my legs.

And those
are your
legs.

Legs are **EVERYWHERE.**

Some legs are L O N G.
See them bend when
they walk.

4

Stringy and stretchy, like very TALL stalks.

5

Some legs are little,
and little is fine.

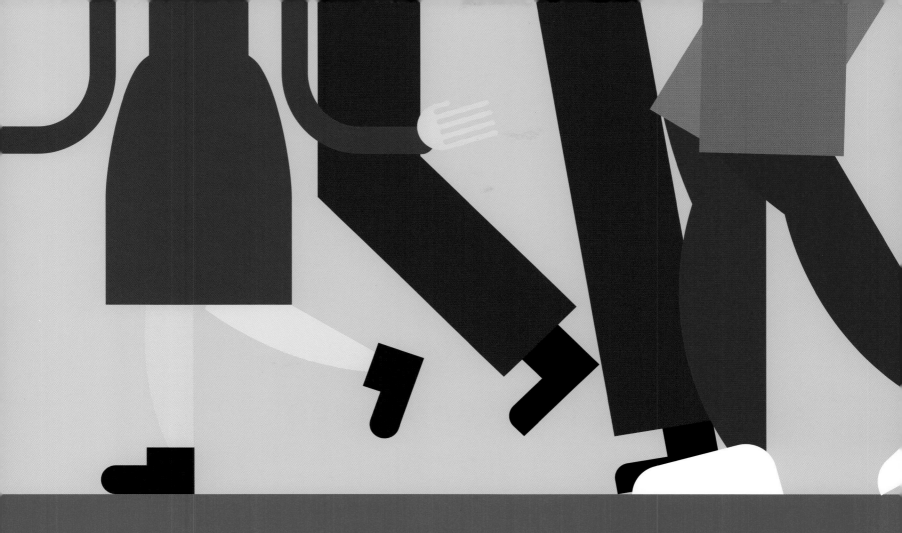

She still wins races
at school all the time.

Some legs are
thin and have
HARD little
knees.

Others are **THICK**, like the trunks of the trees.

9

His feet are small.

See them fit in his shoe.

Her
feet are
BIG.

They just grew and they grew!

11

He cannot WALK,
so to get
over there...

12

Some people
do not have
both of their legs.

14

They might use ones made from metal instead.

15

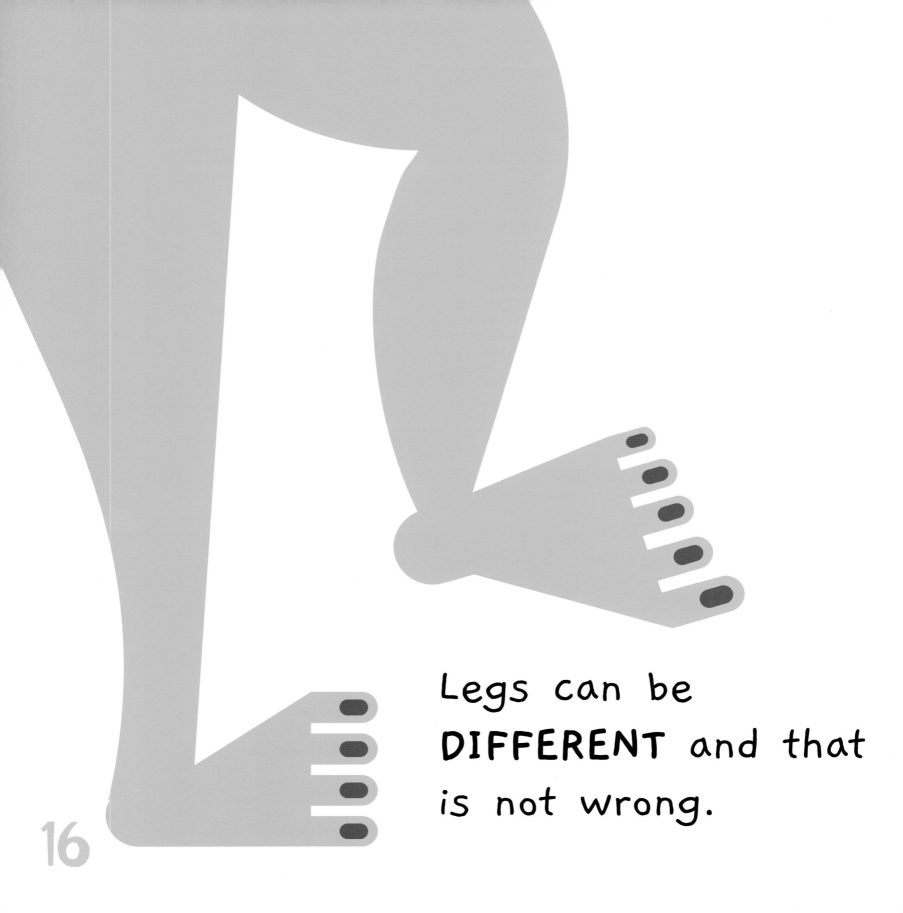

Legs can be **DIFFERENT** and that is not wrong.

16

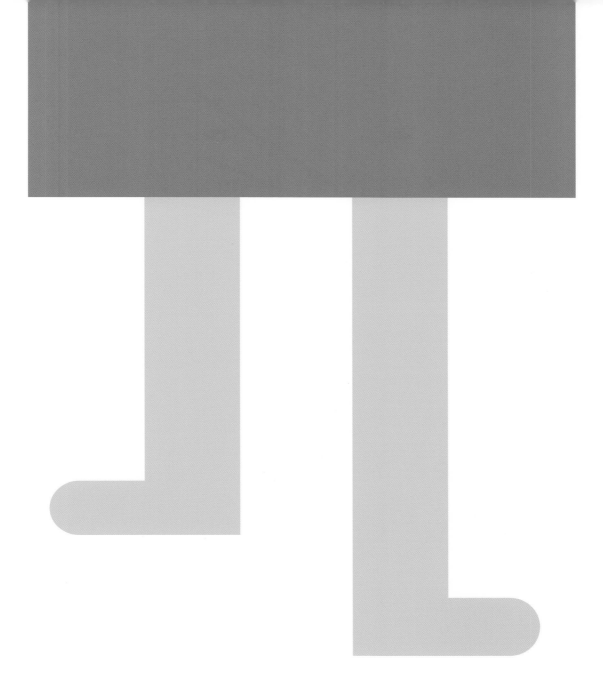

Left can be short and
then right can be long!

Her legs are **STRONG**.
She can kick the ball far.

They like to **DANCE.**
Look how graceful they are!

19

Her legs are **HAIRY**,
right down
to the feet.

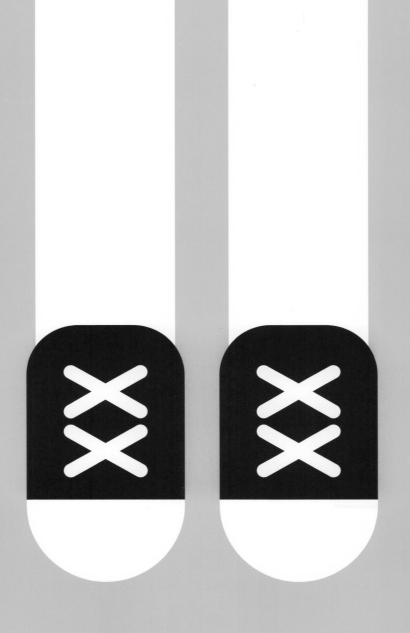

His legs are **SMOOTH** and
as white as a sheet.

21

Legs get less bendy when people get old.

We would go on.
Oh, if only we could!
All legs are **different** and **lovely**
and **good**.

24